Amazon Seller Academy:

A 15-Year Proven Blueprint: How to Sell Stuff on Amazon and Generate Large Semi Passive Income, Retail Arbitrage, Fulfillment by Amazon, Private Label Products and Drop Shipping

Eric Michael

Amazon Seller Academy

Copyright © 2016 Eric Michael. All rights reserved worldwide

© Almost Free Money, Volume 9

This publication is protected under the US Copyright Act of 1976 and all other applicable international, federal, state and local laws, and all rights are reserved, including resale rights: you are not allowed to give or sell this Guide to anyone else.

Please note that much of this publication is based on personal experience and anecdotal evidence. Although the author and publisher have made every reasonable attempt to achieve complete accuracy of the content in this document, they assume no responsibility for errors or omissions. Also, you should use this information as you see fit, and at your own risk. Your particular situation may not be exactly suited to the examples illustrated here; in fact, it's likely that they won't be the same, and you should adjust your use of the information and recommendations accordingly.

Any trademarks, service marks, product names or named features are assumed to be the property of their respective owners, and are used only for reference. There is no implied endorsement if we use one of these terms.

Finally, use your head. Nothing in this Guide is intended to replace common sense, legal, medical or other professional advice, and is meant to inform and entertain the reader.

Amazon Seller Academy

Welcome back friends!

In *this book,* we will discuss current trends in the online sales industry and look at recent updates to the Amazon marketplace to see how they affect store owners.

We will also expand upon several aspects of selling on Amazon that shop owners have asked for more discussion on via Facebook groups and on our blog at http://www.ericmichaelbooks.com/.

There are a number of other books that offer Amazon selling tips on Kindle. Many of these "guides" are ghost-written by "authors" that have never sold an item online. Many of the books cover only one aspect of selling online.

Information products similar to *this book* are being offered online for hundreds of dollars. I do not believe in gouging fellow sellers like that. I provide this information at an extremely affordable cost. In return, all I ask is three things:

1. Leave a positive review on the Amazon book page and on Goodreads.com. The income earned from these books is used for my two boys' college funds.
2. Share this book through your social media outlets and word-of-mouth.
3. Put this information to good use and don't wait to start making money! People who wait for next week usually never end up getting started at all.

In this book, I will explain exactly how I have set up my Amazon storefront for success. Remember, the great thing about the Almost Free Money books is that as soon as you sell that *first additional item,* you have already made profit on your book order! Where else can you say that about any investment?

Life changing benefits gained from reading this book:

1. Take your Amazon shop to the next level and start down the road toward making a full-time income doing what you love.

2. Read about the newest trends on Amazon.com and how they will affect your seller account.

I am excited to share my story with you and get you out there looking for inventory, so you can start making some money. But first, we need to lay out the game plan for this book and discuss reader expectations for the topics that will be covered here.

What you will get from this book:

1. In this book, we are going to start from scratch and build a large Amazon inventory that earns you a significant e-check that goes into your bank account every two weeks (or more often, if you prefer).

Amazon Seller Academy

2. We will go through the basics of selling on Amazon. Even if you have never been on Amazon's website, you will be able to start selling on Amazon. You will know how to list inventory items and process orders (oh... and collect your money from Amazon, too!)

3. I will teach you everything that you need to know to research which types of inventory items to sell. You can figure out for yourself which road is right for you. You should sell in categories that you are familiar with and/or enjoy working in.

4. I will tell you exactly what I have sold on Amazon and why those items worked for me. My 'per-item cost' was only 8 cents an item, the last time that I calculated it. My average sales price was just over $8.50 per item.

5. We will discuss managing your inventory and effective pricing of inventory items, so that your inventory sells quickly and you have more money to increase the size of your inventory.

6. As we proceed through this book, I will provide you with some resources that will help you to build your background knowledge, learn Amazon selling techniques, and find new categories of inventory items in which to sell.

7. You will be introduced to the most popular systems internet sellers use to scale their Amazon into a full time business: Amazon FBA, Private Label Products, drop shipping and wholesaling.

8. A gift of three FREE valuable full-length books, as thanks for ordering the book. These books are all Top 10 Amazon Kindle bestsellers and are included as part of our new Masterclass Instructional Series.

What you will NOT get from this book:

1. A get-rich-quick plan. Although I started selling items within several days of finding my first inventory item, it does take considerable time and effort to build an Amazon inventory that provides a regular and significant passive income. You will also have to re-build your inventory as your items sell. This is a home business, and you will have to work at it to be successful. After reading this book, you will have the advantage of hearing what worked for me, but you will still have to apply the knowledge that you learned and work as hard as I did to build a comparable inventory. Nothing is given to you in this world. If you are not willing to work, do not read any further.

2. This is not an Amazon selling primer. We will cover everything you need to know to build your inventory and maintain your business effectively. But, Amazon does an excellent job of providing Amazon sellers all of the background information that they need to run their business on a day-to-day level. Their Seller Help pages are very easy to understand and navigate. There is also a ton of information online and in other Kindle books for beginning sellers, so this book will not cover that subject in detail.

There. Now we have laid the guidelines for this book. Now let's get the basics out of the way, so we can get to the fun stuff – shopping for great items to put in your Amazon inventory!

Chapter Summary:

Benefits of reading this book:

1. Build a passive income that generates consistent and profitable paychecks
2. Learn Amazon selling basics. Start listing items immediately.
3. How I buy low and sell high on Amazon
4. How to build your Amazon business and manage your inventory for maximum sales
5. Learn how to research new income sources
6. Links to vital how-to pages on the internet
7. Where to network with other sellers – Social Media connections

What this book is not:

1. An Amazon selling instructional book
2. A get-rich-quick book

About The Author

Eric Michael is married and is a proud father of two energetic sons. He enjoys family outings and many outdoor activities, including fishing, hunting and camping.

The information provided in this book and in the Almost Free Money series was compiled during fifteen years of selling goods on the internet from home and related internet research. His personal experiences have developed a unique skill set – the ability to find a diverse selection of free items (or priced under $1) that can be sold on the internet for at surprisingly good profit margins.

Eric Michael was recently featured in Woman's World magazine as an 'Ultimate Expert' regarding selling used items on the internet for profit.

Almost Free Money series books have been #1 Kindle bestsellers in 12 different categories and sold tens of thousands of copies. Currently, there are three AFM books in the Top 10 list in the Auctions and Small Businesses category on Amazon.

Mr. Michael has gone on to develop two popular websites - EricMichaelBooks.com and Garage Sale Academy. He also hosts Facebook fan pages for Almost Free Money and Garage Sale Academy.

'Almost Free Money' books for Internet Resellers:

Amazon Seller Academy

1) Almost Free Money, Volume 1 FREE! (#1 Kindle bestseller, Top 10 for 3 years running). Learn how to find over 500 different types of items for free where you live and sell for profit online and at scrap metal locations for big bucks.
2) Thrift Wars (#1 Kindle Bestseller): Learn how professional sellers locate the best items to resell from thrift stores for very high profit margins. Learn how to sell on Amazon, Etsy and eBay for maximum profit margins.
3) Etsy Empire (#1 Kindle and Softcover bestseller, top 10 for 8 months straight): How to build a powerful Etsy shop and sell handmade and collectible items on Etsy.com. Master Etsy SEO, social media for Etsy and Etsy marketing with a proven step-by-step formula.
4) Etsy Empire Strikes Back (#1 Kindle Bestseller): Advanced techniques for marketing with social media, like Facebook, Instagram and Pinterest, plus the latest Etsy shop rules and updates
5) Almost Free Gold: (#1 Kindle bestseller, top 10 for 12 months straight): Learn how to find valuable gold and silver jewelry for cheap at garage sales and thrift stores. You can also learn how to harvest free gold and silver from junk sources in this fun and unique approach to earning income!
6) The Almost Free Money Triple Play Value Pack: Contains the three bestselling AFM books: Almost Free Money, Passive Income for Life and Garage Sale Superstar. A great bargain!

Amazon Seller Academy

Table of Contents

Business Assessment: Preparing To Succeed	1
Merchant Fulfilled Account: Amazon Selling Basics	3
Ok… Now, How Do I Figure Out What To Sell?	8
How To Build An Impressive Inventory	10
My First Year Of Amazon Selling: Successes And Lessons Learned	16
Categories Of Used Items To Sell	28
Increase Profits And Sell Items Faster By Making Better Item Descriptions On Amazon	37
Pricing And Inventory Management Practices That Yield More Amazon Sales	41
Customer Relations Practices And Maintaining A High Customer Feedback Percentage	47
Diversifying Your Amazon Business: Selling Products On Craigslist, Ebay And Etsy	53
Amazon Fba: An Introduction To Fulfillment By Amazon	56
Retail Arbitrage [Ra]	62
How To Succeed In Ra	68
Introduction To Wholesaling And Private Label Products [Plp]	71
How To Succeed In Wholesale And Plp Systems	75
Introduction To Drop Shipping	78
Preparing To Succeed On Amazon In The Future: Amazon Selling Trends And What They Mean For You	82
Which System Should I Use?	86
Additional Links For Further Research	90
Thank You, Readers!	92

Business Assessment: Preparing To Succeed

If you want to be able to build your pyramid to the very top block hundreds of feet above the other Amazon businesses out there, you need to build a wide and sturdy base for your Amazon pyramid.

The ancient Egyptians did not start building pyramids without developing a plan first, right? Don't you think that they had to figure out how wide to make the structure and how big the blocks would have to be before they started making their slaves move those thousand pound blocks around?

The same principles apply to your Amazon business. Before you start building your pyramid, you have to draw up your blueprint. You must know several things before you start buying inventory for your business.

1. Inventory storage – The amount of space that you have to store your inventory often dictates the types of items that you will buy for your inventory. If you live in an apartment, you will be limited to selling items that do not take up a lot of room, such as media items. You will be looking for items like CDs and books that can be shelved or placed in boxes while they are in your inventory.

We are lucky. We have a good portion of our finished basement in which to store inventory items. We have a 20 x 6' area that houses our music inventory shelves, seven cupboards full of collectibles, board games, and shipping supplies, and also a utility room that is used for storing large inventory items.

2. What types of items do you want to sell? Before you start shopping for inventory items, it is important to know what your main source of income is going to be. This should be determined by your background knowledge (which can be enhanced through research) and your enthusiasm for the topic. In my experience, Amazon sellers do MUCH better when they have a passion for the items that they are selling to their customers. These sellers find better products, describe the items more accurately in item descriptions, and take more care in shipping the sold items to customers. This all adds up to receiving better customer reviews and getting more return customers – two of an Amazon seller's best friends!

Chapter Summary:

What to do before you start buying inventory:

1. Determine how much room that you have for inventory storage
2. Decide which types of items that you are interested in selling

Merchant Fulfilled Account: Amazon Selling Basics

If you asked ten random people on the street how they would go about selling a used item, at least seven of them would probably answer: 1) a garage sale or 2) eBay. One of them might say Craigslist.

Very few people know that you can sell used items on Amazon. Many experienced internet sellers do not even know how easy and profitable it is to sell used items on Amazon. Most of your competition is trying to sell used items via eBay auctions, and that market is not as profitable as it used to be. The auction format has lost its appeal to many consumers. Today, many consumers want to locate the item that they want to buy and purchase it immediately rather than place bids and wait a week to see if they won an auction.

EBay does offer fixed price items, but the largest and most recognized internet marketplace is Amazon.com, and it is not even a close competition. The great thing about the way Amazon is set up is that each item offers several different condition ratings for each item. If you have a used book or CD to sell, it will be listed on the same page as new books from the manufacturer in that particular title.

Why is that such a big deal? Many consumers today are looking for the best possible deal available to them. Often they will browse items with the intent of buying a new item. However, when consumers navigate to the item description page, and see that your CD which is listed as 'Used - Like New' costs about half the price of a brand new item, they may opt to buy your used CD over the pricier new CD listing.

Keep in mind that it is very possible to regularly find used CDs at yard sales for 25 cents, or even for free, as we will discuss later. Amazon provides even inexperienced sellers the opportunity to consistently sell many different types of items at large profit margins. This is what we will be focusing on in this book. But first, we have to learn how to sell items on Amazon.

The first thing that you will have to do is sign up for an Amazon seller account. The process is self-explanatory. Go to the [Amazon seller webpage](), and fill in the required information. You will be providing Amazon your financial information for a checking or saving account, which your earning disbursements will be deposited into on a regular basis. The process is secure. You do not need to worry about providing your information over the internet, if you have not done so before. Amazon is a huge corporation with thousands of individual seller accounts, and they take their information security very seriously.

You will be provided two options from which you must select the type of Amazon seller account that you want to have – Individual Seller or Professional Seller.

By default, you start with an Individual Seller selling account. With the basic selling account, you can list inventory items for free. When your item sells, Amazon credits your account with the amount that you chose to price your item at, minus several fees.

If you sold a book priced at $10 from your basic selling account, you would be charged an 8-20% Amazon finder's fee, a closing fee of about $1.35, and a 99 cent per-item fee. You are then credited with a shipping credit, which varies by item type. This shipping credit often results in the closing fee being covered, as you are given a $3.99 shipping credit for books, for example. Most books cost under $3 to actually ship via USPS.

Once you build a medium sized inventory and you believe that you will be regularly selling at least forty items a month (this will not take you long), you should opt out of the basic selling account and upgrade to the Professional seller account.

The Professional seller account has several major perks. First, the 99 cent per-item fee is waived for all items sold. Second, Professional sellers have the ability to make their own item description pages and add them to the Amazon marketplace. I use this functionality quite often for rare high-end collectibles. The Professional account is currently $39.99, and the fee is deducted from your selling account profits. So, you do not have to pay a separate fee by credit card. It is deducted from your Amazon earnings account on a monthly basis. Amazon also currently offers one free month of Professional account service as a trial, which is nice for those sellers who are right at the 40 sales threshold.

After you have signed up for your account, there is a collection of helpful pages for new Amazon sellers at the [Amazon Help Pages]().

You will want to spend some time here, and perhaps print off some pages and make some notes. If you start to feel a little nervous about the processes… DON'T worry! Selling on Amazon is incredibly easy. It is much simpler than selling an item on eBay and twice as fast, once you have gone through the process a couple of times.

Here is the complete process of selling a used item on Amazon:

1) Find the UPC or ISBN number on the bar code of the item that you want to sell. You can also type in the item's text title or description in the search bar.

2) Go to the Amazon home page. Type the UPC or ISBN number into the search bar at the top of the page. Find the item description page for the item that you want to list. In other words, if you are attempting to list a used copy of the CD 'Pearl Jam – 10', find Pearl Jam 10 in the Amazon search results. Click on the link. You will see a page that gives customers the details of the songs on the CD, along with multiple price listings from other Amazon sellers who are trying to sell Pearl Jam 10.

3) On the top right-hand corner of the description page in a dark blue box, you will see 'Do You Have One to Sell? Sell on Amazon. Click there.

4) Provide the condition and a short description of your item, list your price, and make it available for sale.

Congratulations! Your item is now listed on Amazon and in your seller inventory. It took you about 30 seconds to list it, right? Welcome to the power of Amazon.

5) When your item sells on Amazon, you are sent a notice to your registered email address notifying you of the sale, and the customer details, along with the shipping method that they selected.

6) On your Amazon Seller Account page, you will see the sold item(s) listed there. You are provided a link to 'Buy Shipping' for that order. You complete the information for the shipping label, and print out the label with a standard printer. Tape the label on the box and ship it. Bam! Item out, money in your account. Done.

Chapter Summary:

- Amazon has little competition for many used items
- Why used items sell from new item pages
- Links to Amazon Help pages

How to start selling on Amazon:

1. Sign up for Amazon selling account
2. Individual vs. Professional Seller Accounts
3. Explanation of Amazon fees
4. Step by step process for listing an inventory item on Amazon

Ok... Now, How Do I Figure Out What To Sell?

The most important thing that an Amazon seller can do to increase earnings and profit margins earned on inventory items sold is to learn how to research. The learning process should be a continuous effort. Learning about new sources of inventory and methods for improving business procedures should not wane after you become an experienced seller.

The Amazon landscape is always evolving. Technology makes used items obsolete or undesirable. Consumer appetites change and the demand for pop culture media items can decline rapidly. Sellers have to be able to adjust to these changes accordingly. This is where research is vital. As a seller, you have to know what consumers are buying and how much they are willing to pay for items.

There are a variety of places that can help you to determine what types of items are hot, and what other sellers are doing well with.

Social media is probably the easiest way to research current trends. There is a lot of information on Facebook and Twitter. There are groups dedicated to talking about selling on Amazon, and also the eBay Underground Facebook group has a category about selling on Amazon that has active discussions.

Conduct a simple search on Google or Bing search engines for 'sell used items on Amazon tips', or a similar search query and you will have dozens of free sources of information. There are also many Kindle books devoted to the topic.

Our website EricMichaelBooks.com also has many FREE pages that can assist sellers with finding inventory and also learning how to improve listings and develop good business practices. Among the topics with devoted webpages: How to sell on Amazon, Amazon packaging and shipping, how to sell used books, CDs, DVDs, video games, collectibles and used clothes, how to sell Amazon textbooks, how to find the best items at garage sales, thrift stores, and flea markets. There are also many links provided that direct readers to the best free niche sites related to selling used items.

Chapter Summary:

- The value and importance of research
- Demand for Amazon items changes frequently

Where to start researching types of used items to sell

1. Internet searches and search engine queries
2. Social Media
3. Kindle Books
4. www.EricMichaelBooks.com

How To Build An Impressive Inventory

I started selling used items for profit about 15 years ago. At that time, there was significantly less competition. It was easy to find treasure at garage sales and sell the items on eBay for excellent profit margins.

For the first five years of my business, I sold primarily used collectibles and media items on eBay, and I did well. Over time, several things happened. #1, I got tired of spending all of my time making eBay auctions, and #2, profit margins on eBay shrank as more and more internet sellers discovered how easy it was to sell used items and collectibles on eBay.

It became harder and harder to find quality collectibles at second-hand locations and eBay was getting tougher to sell effectively on. Besides that, eBay continually increased their selling fees and changed their customer feedback structure so that it made it very hard to keep your seller feedback rating high unless you were a high volume seller.

Many collectible item auctions were also ending without a bid. I got tired of paying eBay listing fees, and getting little in return, in many cases. So, I started looking for other ways to diversify my used item sales. Almost immediately, I discovered selling used items on Amazon.

When I first started selling on Amazon, very few sellers sold used items there. As a matter of fact, very few internet sellers even knew that it was possible to sell used items on Amazon.

Heck yeah, I thought. Amazon is a huge marketplace, with less competition than on eBay, and you don't even have to pay listing fees (as on eBay). Let's do this!

My only concern at the time was trying to decide if my efforts would be worthwhile, because I did not know if there would be sufficient demand on Amazon for the used items that I was finding at garage sales, thrift stores, and other second-hand locations.

I started by doing a lot of browsing on the Amazon marketplace.

If you are new to selling on Amazon, it is vital for you to do the same thing that I did. How does spending hours surfing on Amazon help you to sell more items? You get an excellent feel for which categories of items you can make high profit margins in. You learn which types of used items can be sold effectively on Amazon.

I looked at many, many categories of items, and I looked at a lot of individual item pages. I took notes on which categories had used items that were highly priced, and which categories were flooded with used items and therefore not worth my time.

I also noted which types of used items sold very slowly on Amazon. One very helpful feature that you can use to gauge the popularity of items and determine how quickly you can expect to make a sale is the Amazon 'Best Seller's Rank' on each item's description page. This ranking is displayed about halfway down the item page. You will find ranks of anywhere from single digits down to over one million for some rare books. The lower the best seller rank is, the faster the item will typically sell.

How are ranks used to decide what types of items to buy? They provide you with an idea of how long you can expect items to stay on your inventory shelves before you sell them.

Nothing is written in stone. You may find a very rare book that has a Best Sellers Rank of 320,000 and have a collector buy it the same day. However, it is more likely that the book will go unsold for at least several months. Or, it may never sell at all.

Should you buy the book with the rank of 320K? That depends on several things.

If you can buy the book for $1, and you know that the lowest Amazon price listed by other sellers is $80, then obviously it would be worth it to buy the book and list it into your inventory. For that profit margin, I would let that book sit on my shelf for years!

I prefer to have a range of best seller ranks in my inventory. I like to have some items that sell fairly quickly (low best seller rank numbers), so I have liquid funds that I can use to buy more inventory items.

It is also perfectly acceptable to me to have a fairly high percentage of my items ranked in the tens of thousands or higher, as long as the list price is high. Those $80-100 sales of rare items that occur periodically are nice chunks of change, and you WILL find these rare items regularly at second-hand locations, once you know what to look for.

Of course, the amount of slow sellers that you will be buying will depend on how much storage room you have for your inventory. If you do not have much shelving, you may not be able to buy as many large items or rare items that will probably take months to sell. You will have to buy more quick sellers that get sold regularly and get shipped out, which makes room in your inventory for new arrivals.

When I was researching how to start selling used items on Amazon, I also read all of the Frequently Asked Questions for New Amazon Sellers, and I became familiar with the listing and shipping procedures. I read most of the Help pages, so I knew what I was doing BEFORE I started listing items into my inventory.

Once I was done with that, I started figuring out which types of items I would be looking to buy at second-hand locations and then sell on Amazon.

I was amazed at how many types of used items could be sold on Amazon. Media items like books and music have always been Amazon's bread-and-butter. Used media items are easy to find for cheap and they do very well. However, I learned that I could also sell used toys, games, electronics, components, rechargeable batteries, housewares, holiday décor, and much more! In fact, most of these used items were selling for significantly higher prices on Amazon than on eBay, and not many existing Amazon sellers were selling used items in these categories.

Because I had already been selling used items on eBay for five years or so, I knew the types of used items that I routinely found at garage sales and thrift stores, and the price I could typically buy them for. Now, after doing my research, I had a good idea of which types of used items I could sell on Amazon, how long they would take to sell on average, and the profit margin that they would yield when they sold.

My forte has always been finding used items for under $1 and selling them for high profit margins. Initially, I built a very nice inventory of used and collectible books. 95% of these books I bought for 25 to 50 cents at garage sales. Many of these books I actually found in Free Boxes. More details about finding high value Amazon items for free can be found on our website, on a dedicated webpage.

I sold a lot of these 25 cent books for $20-50. We will talk about how to maximize your return on specific types of items later in this book.

Chapter Summary:

How I started building my $50,000 Amazon business

- Prior experience selling on other sites
- How I found Amazon
- What types of used items to sell on Amazon

- Read the Amazon Help pages for sellers

My First Year Of Amazon Selling: Successes And Lessons Learned

The most important thing for an Amazon seller to do is to BUILD UP AN INVENTORY. It is important to be patient. You WILL sell some items for good profits in your first several months of Amazon selling, but it is more important to get a supply of high-yielding items into your inventory. These will often take some time to sell.

Remember, as you add more items to your inventory, you are building your business. Your business will provide you a nice passive income for years. Once you build a large Amazon inventory, your used item business will make money every day. You will even make money while you sleep and while you are on vacation! Awesome, right?!

In my first year of building my Amazon business, I concentrated on keeping expenditures very low. I bought a <u>bunch</u> of books and CD's for 25 cents and under at yard sales. I also got a lot of books for free from family, friends, my home, and at garage sales in free boxes.

One thing that worked in my favor was that the used items that sold the best on Amazon were very easy to find. I spent at most ten hours a week locating inventory items and another couple of hours listing items on Amazon. Usually, I hit garage sales and yard sales on Friday and Saturday mornings. When I started, almost all of my

Amazon inventory items were found at garage sales. Most of these items were ten cents or a quarter.

Usually, I tried to visit at least twenty garage sales a weekend. I put all of my items that I found in boxes, and then listed them on Amazon later in the week while I watched TV. How's that for a tough job, eh? Going to garage sales and making money while you watch TV – still sounds pretty good to me, even after 15 years in this business.

Keep in mind that this was before the days of Smart Phones and Price Checker apps. It was fun listing the items that I had found to see how much profit I was going to make on each one when it sold on Amazon. Almost every weekend, I would find several books worth at least $50. I would also have to discard some books because they were "penny books" on Amazon, due to oversaturation of that title on the Amazon marketplace. I collected all of my penny books, and then I either listed them as large lots of books on eBay for $10, or took them to Goodwill for a tax write-off.

After several weeks of building my Amazon inventory, I had already outgrown my two large bookshelves that I had initially dedicated to housing my Amazon books.

So, that brings us to the first and most important thing that I learned during my first month of Amazon selling: **You HAVE to have an inventory management system**. It saves you a ton of time if you know exactly where your inventory items are, so that when your item sells, you can immediately find your item for shipping.

If I knew then what I know now, I would have developed my system before I started buying inventory, and I would have set up my storage area to allow for a much larger inventory. The more room that you have for your business' inventory to expand, the less hassle you will have down the road.

It would have saved me a lot of wasted time and shuffling items around full bookshelves, which is a real chore. I had to add buy and add bookshelves several different times in the first couple of months. Then, I had to move books around a lot to get them to fit on my existing shelves.

I spent too much time organizing, when I could have been out buying more inventory items. That was part of my learning process.

Take my word for it. Find a way to dedicate a fairly good sized storage area to your Amazon inventory, and make sure that you have at least five large shelving units and/or cupboards to store items in. You will fill them up quickly.

I started with two 5' tall bookshelves, and I easily filled them within a month. Now, our inventory consists of ten 5' x 3' shelves, four large cupboards, and another storage area full of inventory items, and we have downsized recently.

Many Amazon sellers mark their shelves or storage units with a designated number or letter combination, and then note that number in each Amazon listing, so that they can quickly find the item when it sells.

Anything that can save you minutes or even seconds each time you process an Amazon sale should be strongly considered. Keep in mind that over the course of your business, you will probably process tens of thousands of orders. This time you have saved by organizing properly adds up quickly, and the time you save can be spent doing other things, like enjoying time with your family.

When you are setting up your storage and packaging areas, consider organizing them so that you eliminate as much wasted time as possible. Keep your storage and packing areas as close together as possible. Make sure that you can find inventory items immediately, without having to search through multiple shelves. Ensure that storage areas are well-lit so that you can see the titles of your media items. Keep your packing area organized, so that you know where to find the correct sized boxes for packaging items for shipment.

Another concept that helped me out a lot in my first year of Amazon selling was to **start selling what I already knew about and enjoyed looking for**. Because I had already been selling books on eBay for five years, the transition to Amazon was as smooth as silk. I already knew which books were worth buying at garage sales, how to describe books and their specific condition issues, and how to store and ship books.

By selling types of items that you are familiar with, you lower the learning curve and increase the probability of finding valuable items. It also helps a great deal to enjoy what you sell. I know… that sounds like it should be common sense, but there are many internet sellers who choose their genres based only on profit. These types of sellers often burn out quickly or bounce around from genre to genre, never mastering any single category of items.

But, I digress. Let's get back to the story line. By the end of the first month or so, I had filled about two and a half 5 x 3' shelves with books. My Amazon inventory contained about 850 books and I had only spent about $30 of my money and spent about 50 hours of my spare time to get the inventory listed and shelved.

My average list price during my first month was between $4-5. If you figure that the average price spent to buy that inventory was only about 6 cents an item, the profit margin was still excellent. During that first month, I listed a lot of my own books on Amazon, and I got quite a few more of my family's excess books for free. That was why the cost was only 6 cents per item.

After the first month of selling used books on Amazon, sales fluctuated from week to week. The first week I sold a couple of books, and then I sold nothing during week two. The third week, I believe I sold at least ten books, and that was when I started selling a couple of higher value books ($40-50), as well.

The point that I am trying to make is that it takes a while to start making profit. Do not expect to start selling items immediately, unless you choose a category that has a high demand, such as newer video games (which will cost you significantly more money to build your inventory).

In most cases, the number of sales and also the consistency of your sales will mirror your inventory numbers. You will not start seeing a constant flow of sales until you build your inventory to a sufficient level, and that level is determined by your choice(s) of inventory items.

For me, it took about three months of steady building to an inventory of about 2,000 items before sales really started to roll in consistently. It was also nice to hit that inventory level because items were starting to move off of my shelves faster as they sold on Amazon.

By then, I was getting a lot better at picking "winners". My per-item average rose significantly (probably doubled) by the third month. So, as some of the books I had listed in the first couple of weeks were finally selling and getting shipped out, I was able to replace them with higher value books, which raised the average list price. Woo hoo!

From about the third month on, I knew that I could make consistent money selling used items on Amazon. I started to look for ways to diversify my inventory. We will discuss the pros and cons of diversification in a later chapter, but suffice it to say, I don't like having all of my eggs in one basket. That was one of the reasons I started researching other sources of cheap inventory for my Amazon business.

Having a number of different things to look for while I was "picking" also made looking for inventory at yard sales more fun. I started adding items like: CDs, video games, board games and used toys.

At about that same time, I shifted from picking primarily at garage sales to spending a significant amount of time at thrift stores and second-hand stores. Thrift stores are akin to visiting one hundred garage sales, all under one roof!

I saved a lot of gas money by only driving to one or two locations, instead of forty. The condition of the items is also much better at thrift stores, as employees only place items of at least a decent quality on their shelves. The other donated junk (which you often see at yard sales) gets tossed in the dumpster.

Thrift stores provide the opportunity to find some excellent high-value items, especially in areas where there is not an overabundance of Amazon sellers. Some items have a lot of competition in most thrift stores (books, for instance). But, if you do your research on diversifying types of inventory items, you will have a leg up on 90% of the other sellers who focus only on the easy items, like books.

Thrift stores also require a bit more experience and patience than garage sales. At garage sales, many items are underpriced. At thrift stores, the used items usually cost more to buy, so you have to be careful that you can make a minimum profit on each item.

It is easy to lose money on items bought at thrift stores. It did not take me many visits to the local thrift shop to figure out that I had better be careful buying hardcover books for $2! I was finding several $20 hardcover books, but I was also taking some hits on some penny books. Again, this was before the advent of the Smart phone, which now allows you to check current Amazon prices using a bar code scanner and/or photograph of the book that you are considering for purchase.

Thrift stores are also time savers. If you have limited time, you can pick dozens of items at a thrift store in under an hour. Thrifts also provide you the opportunity to shop during the week and after work. Garage sales limit you to picking on the weekends, when often, you would rather be doing other recreational activities with your family or friends.

During the fourth or fifth month of Amazon selling, I also started looking for large lots of items to break up and sell as single items on Amazon. I found a lot of good deals on eBay on large boxes of books. It was common to find 25-50 item lots of books on eBay five years ago for cheap. At that time, there were a lot of eBay sellers who only sold books on that website and not on Amazon.

I routinely found valuable book titles in those large lots that paid for the entire lot all by themselves. All of the other books were gravy. It was obvious that the seller had tried to list all of the books on eBay, and then threw them all into a lot after they did not get a bid on eBay. Many rare books do not get bid on within one week on an eBay auction because few eBay bidders are looking for that particular subject. The eBay seller's loss is the Amazon seller's gain.

I found a lot of $20-30 books buried in $5 eBay book lot auctions. Even after paying for the shipping fees, I often listed over $100 worth of profit. Obviously, not every lot was a winner, but I won much more than I broke even. I also won a lot of single book auctions at the minimum bid of $1, and then listed the same book on Amazon for over $20.

Many of the auctions that I was bidding on had misspelled titles, were listed in the wrong category, or had very poor item descriptions and photographs. In some cases, I even flipped the same book back onto eBay with a good description and multiple photos, and turned some quick and significant profits.

I also finally "went big" during the fifth month. I found a deal that I couldn't pass up, while I was searching through bulk book lots on eBay. An eBay seller had listed about a thousand books that did not sell at her garage sale. The eBay auction only had a couple of minutes left and had not received a bid for $50.

My initial thought was… 'My wife would kill me. Where would we put 1,000 more books?!'

I decided to take a risk. At a penny or two a book, how could I lose, right?

To make a long story short, I won the auction for $50, and had to drive for three hours and pick up about 1200 pounds of books in our lightweight S.U.V. and rickety trailer. I had to load up all of the books myself, as my wife had to watch the kids at home (and she was pissed – ha!). I sweated all of the way home, hoping that the weight of the books did not overheat the truck's engine, or break the axle on the old trailer.

Well, five hours later, I rolled into the driveway, and I unloaded all of the book boxes into our basement. Sheesh. The boxes filled half of the basement. Anyway, I went through all of the books, and there were a lot of penny books in the lot… but, there was also an $80 book that sold several months later, and five or six $50 books. There were also another 80 books that I listed on Amazon for $3-20. All in all, I probably listed $600-700 worth of books into my Amazon inventory.

It actually was more time and work than I liked to get rid of the rest of the books, but I made another couple of hundred dollars by grouping categories of books together and then listing them as book lots on eBay. I also sold several other single books on eBay for another $50, or so. It was a pretty good investment for a $50 auction and $50 in gas. I almost made the eBay auction investment back with one $80 book sale!

Several months later, I bought a 10,000 item music lot on eBay for $700. This was the steal of the decade! I ended up listing over 12,000 items on Amazon (there were considerably more items than were advertised) at an average price of over $8.50 each. There were a lot of rare CDs and vinyl records in that lot. I also sold another hundred items on eBay.

By the time I had listed all of the items in that lot six months later, I had jump-started my Amazon business. My inventory jumped from a modest 1,500 items to over 11,000 items, and the average price stayed at about $8 an item.

Yes, I had to rent a U-Haul trailer and haul the lot from five hours away. I also lost the use of my garage and part of my basement for several months and my wife and I spent a lot of free time listing items on Amazon.

But, by the time all of the items were listed on Amazon, I went from selling 4-5 items on Amazon for $50 a week to selling 10-20 items a week for a consistent $300-$700 and considerably more around Christmas.

There you have it. The true story of how I built a $50,000-$70,000 Amazon inventory in my spare time. By buying used items at garage sales, thrift stores, and online and large bulk lots of goods, I kept my expenditures at a very minimal level for the projected return.

I was able to build my Amazon business in my spare time at my own pace. A lot of the "work" was done after working at my full-time job during the day, and then settling down on the couch or on the deck and while enjoying a cool beverage.

Now, I have built an Amazon business that will continue to pay for my efforts for a long time, with very little maintenance. You have to love passive income! Down the line, I may also opt to sell my Amazon business for $30-50K, and make a down payment on a vacation home. We will see what happens!

Chapter Summary:

What I learned in my first year of Amazon selling:

- The most important thing is not initial sales. Start building your inventory and worry about the number of sales later.
- Start by getting used items for free or buying at very low prices
- Sell free items that you already have in your home
- Look for 'high-profit' items
- Buy cheap items at garage sales and thrift stores.
- Look for large lots of low priced items to break up into single Amazon inventory items
- Flipping eBay listings to Amazon – Lots and Single items

Categories Of Used Items To Sell

I would like to talk to you about what to look for while you are shopping for inventory items at garage sales, yard sales, flea markets and thrift stores and provide you with some tips that will help you to find high value items at very low prices.

Books:

Books are easy to sell on Amazon and can be very profitable, which is why so many existing Amazon sellers specialize in selling them. Books are available at almost every yard sale and thrift store, and they are usually affordable. Plus, some older books are collectible and valuable. You will regularly find $20 books wherever you look for Amazon inventory.

The EMB Used Books page has many tips for how to find high priced books to add to your inventory, but here are some highlights:

- Use a Smart Phone with the Amazon Price Check application. This takes the guess-work out of deciding which used books to buy for profit. You scan the book with your Smart phone, and the app tells you what the book is selling for on Amazon.
- Used textbooks can be sold for excellent profits. If you have bought textbooks lately,

you know that even used texts can cost $150. But, you have to be careful buying textbooks without the Amazon Price Check app. Many titles are updated yearly, so if you have a textbook that is two or three years old, it may be outdated and worthless.

- Many sellers look for hardcover books and textbooks to sell for profit, but I have well over 100 softcover books in my Amazon inventory worth over $50, and several over $100. Look for rare titles, softcover texts, vintage pulp fiction titles, and very thin books. Many of these vintage books with less than 40 pages are rare and collectible.
- If you look at a book and think "Who in the heck would want to read that?!" it is probably rare and valuable. Buy it. Some of the highest priced books in my inventory are not first edition classics, they are rare paperbacks: Flood Hazards in Virginia - $195, The Thrift Store Prospector - $195.60, Answers to the Space Flight Challenge - $145. All three of these books are thin vintage softcover books found for under $1.
- Condition is very important. Books with condition problems like broken hinges, missing pages, and modern books with missing dust jackets can make the books worthless for resale.
- Check all free boxes at yard sales for books and media items. Take EVERY book that

you can find for free. The worst case scenario is that you have to donate the items to Goodwill later. I have found many $20 books in free boxes.

Music:

Used music such as CDs, vinyl records and even 8-tracks, cassettes, and other vintage formats can be sold on Amazon. Some collectible vinyl record and CD titles can be worth thousands of dollars, but it is very rare to find these at second-hand stores.

Selling used music is a competitive business. Everybody loves music. Still, you can make good money selling used CDs and records, if you know what to look for and how to sell them. Many used music internet sellers hang out on eBay for some reason, which gives Amazon sellers a big advantage.

Amazon allows you to list inventory for free. EBay also has tens of thousands of used music items at auction at any given time. Tons of quality items never get bids on eBay. The same item can be listed for free on Amazon, sell for a higher price, and sellers are given a $3.99 shipping credit.

Here is a selection of helpful tips for buying used music for profit:

- Don't be tempted to buy music that you like for $2+. Many popular titles on CD are 'penny CDs'. Remember, millions of these CDs were printed, and many CDs are being tossed in favor of MP3 files.

There is an overabundance of many pop titles at second hand locations and on Amazon, which makes many excellent used CDs almost worthless to sell on Amazon.

- Use Amazon Price Check app.
- Look for rare CDs, and classical titles. Vintage blues and jazz CDs can also be valuable.
- Pick up any CDs that are sealed and you can sell on Amazon as 'New'.
- Grab any CDs that you see in free boxes. Even CDs without cases can be sold on Amazon.
- Check all CDs before you buy them. Ensure that the CD is in the case, as thieves often steal the disc and leave the case, especially at thrift stores. Also, check for large surface scratches, missing artwork, and broken case hinges.
- Keep a supply of replacement cases on hand. I often swap out cases with broken hinges, broken CD holders, or surface cracks.

Video Games and DVDs

Used video games can be excellent sellers on Amazon! It is common to find used video game systems for $10 or less at second-hand locations, and many vintage systems will sell for $30-70 when packaged with the cords, controllers and a couple of games.

It would be well worth your time to scan through the video game system category on Amazon, so that you have a good idea what each system is currently selling for.

Become familiar with what the power cords and AV cords for video game systems look like, so you can pick them up when you see them at garage sales or thrift stores. I have found a lot of cords for 25 cents at garage sales, packed in with big bags of cords at thrift stores, and even in free boxes. You never know when you will find a system that is missing a cord.

Just last week, I found an original PlayStation at a thrift store for $4. It had no cords or controllers with it, which is why it was priced so cheaply. I took it home, dug through my 'random cords box', and found a PlayStation 1 power cord, AV cord and two controllers.

I found all of these accessories in free boxes at garage sales over the years. I tested the PlayStation, and it worked great. I listed it on Amazon and it sold yesterday for $25. If I would have had some PS1 games to package with the system, I could have earned another $5 to $10.

Both DVDs and video games are constantly upgrading in technology. The newest video game system titles can bring $40 used and sell the same day that Amazon sellers list them. That is why it can really pay to have your Smart phone with you. These newer video games will not be $1 or $2. But, even if you have to pay $10 for a $30 title with high demand, you win.

DVDs are getting harder to make money on, unless you are selling on Amazon FBA. Many tech-savvy consumers are opting to buy movies by streaming them on their computers and most people now get movies sent to their homes via Netflix.

This is especially true of newer titles that are available in Blu-ray. Many used standard DVDs are penny DVDs, when the same title is now available on Blu-ray.

Look for older DVDs that were not re-released on Blu-ray. Popular TV series DVD sets also sell well. We hit a home run about three years ago when the local hospital gave their nurses free copies of vintage TV show DVD sets. Several of our friends gave us their copies, and we found quite a few more at thrift stores, still in the shrink-wrap. Several of the sets sold for almost $100, and the single episodes sold for $20-30. Bingo!

Some other DVDs to look for: Director's cuts, Collector's Sets of popular titles and classics, Remastered DVDs, rare titles that you have never heard of, cult classics, and vintage sports DVDs. I have also done very well with rare concert DVDs, especially if you can find early concerts of popular bands or punk rock / thrash concerts.

You can also occasionally make some money on rare VHS tapes, but they sell slowly and most of them are not worth much. If you can get them for free... take them, of course.

Used Toys and Board Games:

Selling used toys and games on Amazon is a nice racket. Very few people know that you can sell these used items on Amazon. The great thing is that often, you cannot sell these items on eBay and make a profit, either. So, the few of us Amazon sellers who know about selling used toys on Amazon are the only ones buying these items to sell.

You can sell almost every modern used toy in decent condition on Amazon, as long as you have either A) a bar code or B) the actual name of the toy (which is often more difficult to figure out than you might think).

Pay attention to the toys aisles while you are at Meijer, K-Mart and Wal-Mart so that you know what toys are titled and which toys are expensive to buy at stores. Those are the toys that you will look for while at second-hand stores and garage sales.

Even loose action figures, Hot Wheels, Barbie dolls, and other small toys can be sold in used condition. Used toys can often take some time to sell, but you can also get these toys for very cheap. If you have young kids like we do, outgrown toys can become profit makers in your Amazon inventory, especially large outdoor toys and electronic toys.

We have sold many used toys that our boys have outgrown. Kids also learn about the value of keeping toys in good condition. We let our boys sell their own toys to upgrade to new ones, but the toys that are in poor condition or missing pieces… sorry, boys.

Used board games can also be sold fairly effectively sold on Amazon. Some are worth $50+. In the last couple of years, I have sold four sealed board games found at thrift stores for over $50, including an original Trivial Pursuit for $80 that was sold in two days. The vintage 3M bookshelf games also sell for good profits – usually over $20.

Some other games to look for: Electronic board games, vintage versions of classic games and handheld electronic games.

Household and Decorative Items:

As we discussed before, almost anything with a barcode can be sold on Amazon. If you see items at garage sales that are still in the original packaging and it has a barcode, it can be listed in seconds and will probably yield good profits.

I have sold a wide array of used household items found at garage sales and thrift stores. Newer decorative items that are sold at popular department stores often sell fairly quickly on Amazon. My wife has even sold new handbags that she bought on clearance at Kohl's, and doubled her purchase price on almost every Amazon sale.

Some categories of items that I have sold on Amazon and made good money: electronics, prints, utensils, clocks, and holiday decorations (Halloween décor sells for higher prices than Christmas, for some reason).

Understand that many used household items sell very slowly, and you will have to store them for a while. Many of these items are larger and bulkier than media items, so you will need more room than you would for books or CDs.

Chapter Summary:

Types of used items that can be found for cheap and sold on Amazon for high profit margins:
- Books
- Music
- Video Games
- Toys and Games
- Household Items
- New sealed items with barcodes

Increase Profits And Sell Items Faster By Making Better Item Descriptions On Amazon

It never ceases to amaze me how lazy some people are. I always look at other sellers' item descriptions while I am listing my own items. There are many sellers who do not even bother to type in a description of their item, or its condition!

A typical Amazon item page will have dozens of listings from sellers. Besides the price, there are only two things that customers can look at to determine which Amazon seller that they will buy the item from.

The first is the seller's rating, which is displayed beside the seller's name. We will talk about seller ratings and your reputation on Amazon later.

The second thing that Amazon customers look at is the item description.

Keep in mind that there are typically multiple listings that will be priced within $1 of each other, so the item description is often what sells the item to the costumer. Still, there many listings that do not have a description at all, just a condition listing and price.

For us small to medium sized Amazon sellers, that is a huge advantage. Many companies with huge inventories do not take the time to make effective item descriptions. By spending less than 30 seconds, you can set your listing apart from the other listings and make it much more likely to sell.

Let's take this step by step, using an example. We will list a copy of "The Hobbit" that I have in my personal collection for sale on Amazon.

1. First, we find the correct Amazon item page. There are many versions of The Hobbit, so we will enter a text description – 'The Hobbit 1967 hardcover'. We scan through the search results and find the exact title, with the same dust jacket art that we want to sell. Select that listing
2. Look through the existing listings from other sellers and determine the price that you want to sell your copy for. I usually price my items at the low end of the listings for each item condition. In other words, for "The Hobbit", there will be many listings for each condition subcategory. The lowest existing price for my book in the 'Used – Very Good' subcategory is $8.85. I may list my book at $8.80.
3. Start your item description by verifying that the copy that you have is the exact item for that description page. This gives customers confidence that they are getting exactly what they want. My description would start with this: 'The Hobbit by Tolkien, 1967 hardcover book with dust jacket. 2nd

Edition, 4th Print, illustrated. Dust jacket art as seen above'.

4. Describe the condition of the book. Do not rely on the Amazon condition guidelines. Most customers do have any idea what the guidelines are. Remember, your reputation is at stake, so make sure that your customers know what they are buying. The second part of the description would be: 'Interior VG. No marks, missing pgs, etc. Jacket G –several chips at edges, one repaired split to back. No other stickers, marks. Binding like new.'

5. Give the customer even more confidence by giving them a short sales pitch. This should be saved as a text document, so that you can cut-and-paste it into each Amazon listing: 'Reliable and experienced book seller with thousands of satisfied customers. Items are securely packaged using dedicated book mailers in bubble wrap. International and Expedited orders welcome.'

This whole listing would take you no more than 20-30 seconds to type and/or cut-and-paste. Yet, this listing will make your item much more likely to sell to the first couple of customers looking to buy "The Hobbit" in used condition.

One thing to note is that you only have a certain amount of characters that will be displayed to buyers on the initial item page. If you have a long description, only the first part of the description will be seen, and the customer would have to click on the 'More' link to see the rest of the description.

Try to get the most important information displayed on the initial screen. Make sure that verification of the item and the most important condition description(s) are visible from the item listing page, without the customer having to click anything.

If the customer is interested in your item listing, they will usually click on the 'More' link to read the rest of your description.

Chapter Summary:

It is important to write good item descriptions
- Earn more sales by building customer confidence
- Prevent non-positive customer feedback

What does a good Amazon item description contain?
1. Verify item – Identification numbers, titles
2. Thorough condition description(s)
3. Build confidence in your business – safe shipping, experience
4. Keep important information first

Pricing And Inventory Management Practices That Yield More Amazon Sales

Let's face it. Most people who buy used items do so in order to save some money over buying new items. What does that mean for the used item seller on Amazon?

In my opinion, you must price items to move. That means that many items should be priced at the lower end of the price range for the applicable condition subcategory for each item that is listed. About 75% of my inventory items are the lowest priced item in their condition subcategory.

On the surface, this may seem to be counterproductive to profits. Really, this strategy works well for several reasons. Number one, impulse buyers are going to pick the lowest priced used item that they are looking to buy, even if your item has a couple of minor condition issues. Number two, customers who choose the lowest priced items are not as picky as the customers who choose to upgrade to higher priced offerings. You will have fewer customer returns and negative feedbacks from customers who buy the lowest priced item that is offered.

This does not mean that if you have a high-priced collectible that is in excellent condition that you should lose profits by listing your item at a price that is cheaper than inferior products. This 'lowest price principle' only applies to identical items that are comparable in condition.

One trick that I have used for rare items with only a couple of listings is to set the price far above the lowest price. For instance, if I have a rare CD that only has one other listing at $4.99; I will often list my copy at $24.95. I have sold many items at the higher price using this method, as long as the description identifies the item well and specifies that it is collectible and rare. Sometimes, the $24.95 item will even sell before the $4.95 item, because the customer thinks that there is something wrong with the lower priced item. Even if the lower priced item sells first, you will still have the next lowest priced item at $24.95, so the next customer will have no choice – your $24.95 item, or nothing. This method works great.

Professional Seller Account owners have the ability to make additions to the Amazon marketplace for items that are not available on the Amazon marketplace. I have made hundreds of these additions for rare books, vinyl records, CDs and other collectibles. The process is easy. You enter details for the item, upload a digital photograph, and then describe your item condition to list it into your inventory. Amazon required almost all new listings to have a UPC bar code, so I purchase UPCs on eBay at a price of 1,000 UPCs for under $4.

If I have to make an addition, I assume that the item is rare (or it would have already been on the Amazon marketplace, right?). If I have to add an item page on Amazon, I never price the inventory item below $20. Often, I will price the item at $50 or $100. Usually, even when other Amazon sellers list their items on item pages that I have added, they will price their items based on my price – perhaps $1 under mine.

More often than not, if you have to make a sales page, nobody will find a copy of that item for a long time. I have sold many items that I have made listing pages for between $50 and $100. Sometimes, they sell quickly, as if people were looking for the item, but had previously been unable to find one.

You will have to manage your inventory periodically to keep your prices competitive with other sellers' listings. After you have been adding items for a while, you will find that items that you listed as the lowest prices item in its condition subcategory are $1 or $2 above the lowest price. It is very common for other sellers to do exactly what you do… set the lowest price by condition.

There are three ways that you can look at this situation. Number one, you can take an aggressive pricing tact, and use Amazon's 'price match' option. There is a check-box on each listing page that allows you to match the lowest price by item, or by condition subcategory. You can use this option for some higher priced items, but be careful using it for low priced items. All it takes is for one idiot to price their item at a penny. Then you are stuck only making a couple of cents on the shipping credit, if somebody buys your item for a penny because of the price match.

The second pricing approach is to set your own price and not adjust it, regardless of what other sellers do. This approach also has risks. You will lose some $50 sales to other Amazon sellers, when they undercut your low price by a penny. Despite the risks of losing some sales, this is the easiest approach to use for experienced sellers with large inventories. Besides, you have an advantage over many of your competitors if you write item descriptions as we have discussed and observe the customer relations advice in the next chapter (you will have higher ratings than most used items sellers).

The third approach is a hybrid between the two approaches that we have already talked about. With this approach, you adjust your item prices periodically. Most of the time, you will be reducing your price by only a couple of pennies, but you will be the lowest priced item again. You will get the most sales on Amazon if you are the lowest priced used item.

Using this approach, you MUST force yourself to adjust your prices according to a schedule, as adjusting your prices is the most boring and time consuming task Amazon sellers have to do. Finding inventory is enjoyable. Listing items at good prices is rewarding. Adjusting your inventory prices sucks, but it is beneficial.

By the time you get to several thousand items in your inventory, it will take you a long time to adjust the prices of all of your items. Adjusting prices is easy. You go to your 'manage inventory' under the 'inventory' tab. Then, you only have to change the prices from the list and click Save. You do not have to access individual item pages to adjust their prices. However, when you have to change hundreds or thousands of items, it can take a very long time.

You can also update several pages of inventory prices at a time, rather than adjusting your entire inventory at once. Using this method, you will not keep your inventory prices as current, but it allows you break up the monotony of adjusting your entire inventory at once.

When I began selling on Amazon, I was updating my prices about every other week. It's easy to accomplish the task, when you do not have many inventory items.

Now, I would say that I use a combination of approach #2 and #3. Now that I have an inventory of almost 10,000 items, I have a pretty good flow of inventory items off of my shelves. I know that if I updated my prices more often, I would increase sales. But, updating my inventory would take days, if I were to do it all at once.

Time spent updating my inventory is time that I do not have to find additional inventory items or spend on other projects, like writing books.

With over 10,000 items, I have 40 pages of items with 250 items displayed per page. I tend to update about five pages every other week. Also, I update my entire inventory at least twice a year.

Now that I have been selling on Amazon for a while, I think that my items often sell before other sellers' listings when the prices are comparable, anyway. If customers look at seller stats, they can see that I am an experienced Amazon seller, and my positive feedback percentage is very high for a used item seller. I do not feel that I have to lower prices as much now as I used to when I began selling on Amazon.

Chapter Summary:

How to price your used items: Lowest price in condition subcategory sells more items and turns inventory over to make room for new items.

Approaches for inventory pricing management

1. Maintain the lowest price in the condition subcategory – Price matching
2. Set your best prices when you list items, and leave them
3. Hybrid – Limited price matching

Customer Relations Practices And Maintaining A High Customer Feedback Percentage

There is no difference between the manner in which you should treat a customer at a physical store and the way you should treat Amazon buyers. Keeping your customers happy is vital to your Amazon business. As we discussed in prior chapters, your Amazon positive feedback percentage is one of the first things that your potential customers will look at when deciding whether to buy goods from you.

Let's take a step back and I will explain Amazon's feedback process and what feedback means for your business.

Most people are familiar with the idea of feedback for internet purchases. EBay has been using customer feedback for years and it is integrated into their buying process. Amazon's feedback process is not as prominent in their business model, as Amazon was originally designed primarily for selling new factory-sealed goods, while eBay has always been seen as an outlet for selling used and collectible items.

With the Amazon feedback model, customers are able to leave feedback for every transaction that they complete through Amazon, but feedback is not requested by Amazon. Buyers have to access their customer order page to find the link to leave feedback. Many Amazon buyers do not even know that there is a feedback system for Amazon purchases. I receive customer feedback on less than 10% of my transactions.

Customers often don't think about leaving feedback... unless there is a problem with their order, or they receive an item that exceeds their expectations.

"Listen to me now, and believe me later", as Hans and Franz said in Saturday Night Live... Protect your feedback percentage at all costs. Do NOT take negative and neutral feedbacks lightly. If you do receive negative feedback, make every effort to contact your buyer and come to an agreement whereby they will remove their negative feedback.

Amazon provides a link with every transaction, so that you can contact your buyer. There is also a link provided from your Seller Feedback page. I recommend the following approach when contacting customers... kiss butt.

Whoever said that "the customer is always right" is full of crap. 95% of the time, they are wrong. Most of the time, it is the customer who made the mistake by ordering items from the wrong category or buying items without reading the condition description.

Still, in order to protect your feedback rating, you have to appease jaded customers. Be overly friendly. Apologize. Explain your position without sounding condescending. I have had very good luck using the following process after receiving neutral or negative feedback.

First, contact the customer as soon as possible. With your first message, apologize for any misunderstanding, and ask them what you can do to resolve the situation. If there is a disagreement in the condition described or the item's assigned condition, provide the customer with the condition guidelines and explain why you assigned that condition to the item in question. Explain that assigning conditions is subjective for used items and people often disagree, but that you did your best to describe the condition. Provide them with the [process for removing feedback](), so that they can voluntarily remove the feedback. I cut-and-paste the instructions from the Amazon help page.

If there is still a problem after the initial message is sent, or if the customer does not respond, I send a second message several days later. In the second message, I apologize again, and offer to refund the entire order and not require the customer to send the item back provided they remove their negative feedback. Make sure that you give them the feedback removal instructions again.

Most customers will remove their feedback, especially when you make it financially attractive with the second message. Remember, your feedback rating is very important, and even if you have to take a $20 loss, you will be much further ahead in the long run if you can get a negative feedback removed.

When you sell used items on Amazon, you WILL receive non-positive feedbacks. It is just a question of when it is going to happen. As I mentioned before, even the best sellers of used items get negative feedbacks. This is due in part to the nature of selling used items and the requirement of assigning subjective values, and partly because there are just a number of stupid people out there. Some people just are not going to be happy, no matter what you do. So be prepared to deal with the non-positive feedback(s), because you will receive them eventually.

Here are some steps that you can take to minimize negative feedbacks:

1. Accurately assign condition ratings. When in doubt, assign Used – Good instead of Used – Very Good. Describe condition issues completely in the text description when listing your items.
2. Answer your seller messages, ASAP. Amazon sends you a copy of messages from buyers to your registered email account and you can also view your messages from your Amazon Seller Home page. When you get messages, respond immediately. Nothing pisses off people more than getting ignored.
3. Deal with non-positive feedbacks immediately, using the procedure described.
4. Don't list items with major flaws. I don't buy anything that I think should be rated as 'Used – Acceptable', which is the lowest condition rating. Don't list anything that you would not like to receive in the mail yourself.

5. Put yourself in your potential customers' shoes. What would you want to know about the item before buying it? What aspects of the condition of the item would you want described to you? Make sure that you address these concerns in your item description.
6. Do not list your item in the wrong category! I see this all of the time when listing used vinyl records. Sellers list CDs in the Vinyl Record category because there is not an existing item page for some rare CDs. Not only is this misleading for customers, it is a violation of Amazon policy and you can get banned from selling on Amazon.
7. Package your items securely, so they do not get damaged during shipping.
8. Consider enclosing a message with each item shipped, or send buyers a personal email with your logo on it. Explain how important customer satisfaction is to your business, and ask them to contact you if there are any condition issues prior to leaving feedback. I have always been undecided on whether to send additional messages regarding feedback. On one hand, you are showing your concern for customer satisfaction. On the other hand, you may be creating more problems for yourself by suggesting that there may possibly be issues with your product(s).

Chapter Summary:

It is vital to your Amazon business to keep customers happy!

1. Builds your business' reputation – High feedback rating = more sales
2. Earn return customers and word-of-mouth advertising
3. Reduces item returns and refunds

How to deal with unhappy customers

1. Return e-mails and messages ASAP
2. Kiss butt and show concern for their issue(s)

How to handle non-positive feedback (This is super important!)

1. Immediate e-mail message
2. Kiss butt, apologize, and tell the customer you value their opinion
3. Explain the value of your feedback rating, and how non-positive feedbacks significantly affect your business. Provide the 'Remove Feedback' instructions
4. If #3 does not work, send a second e-mail that offers a full refund and do not require return of the item, in exchange for feedback removal.

Diversifying Your Amazon Business: Selling Products On Craigslist, Ebay And Etsy

A good internet seller does not limit themselves to selling on only one venue. There are many different ways to sell used items and sellers can take advantage of the benefits each location provides.

Although I believe that Amazon is by far the best overall location to sell the types of goods that I sell, there are times when it is easier or more productive to sell my items on sites other than Amazon.

For instance, there are going to be times when you want to sell items with a quick turnaround. Perhaps you have a family vacation coming up, or you want to make a large purchase.

EBay almost guarantees a sale within a week, if you set the starting price low enough to encourage bidding. You can even make your auction shorter to decrease the time it takes to get payment for your items – you can make 3-Day or even 1-Day listings.

EBay also has the following benefits, when compared to selling on Amazon:

1. Often shorter time to get your money – 1 day to 1 week.

2. There is always the potential to have your auction make more money than you thought the item was worth. If you get the right situation and have multiple bidders who really want your item, you can make a lot of extra money.
3. Visually appealing items benefit from additional photos on eBay
4. Some categories of items cannot be sold on Amazon, or sell very slowly. For instance, vintage used clothing can make a lot of money on eBay, but cannot be sold on Amazon.
5. You can set your own shipping fees on eBay. Some items have insufficient shipping allowances on Amazon. You sometimes end up eating profit to make up for the shipping shortage on Amazon.

I use eBay infrequently, but there are definitely advantages to listing items in an auction setting there from time to time.

Etsy.com is another internet location that specializes is vintage items, arts and crafts and craft supplies. Etsy is an excellent location to sell retro and mid-century items, which you can often find at garage sales for cheap. These items can sell for hundreds of dollars on Etsy. Etsy is set up much like eBay Fixed Price listings. You make a listing like on eBay, and provide photos. Your listing is active for 3 months for twenty cents.

For further discussion on the benefits of Amazon, Etsy and eBay, see the Garage Sale Academy page eBay Selling Alternative.

I also use Craigslist for selling large items that would cost too much to ship on Amazon or eBay. Craigslist listings are free, and there is also the advantage to avoiding the hassle of packaging and shipping large or very fragile items.

Chapter Summary:

How and when to diversify your used item sales using other websites
1. eBay – see below
2. Etsy for vintage, retro, and arts & crafts
3. Craigslist for large, heavy, or very fragile items to avoid shipping

When eBay may be a better choice to sell used items:
1. Certain used items cannot be sold effectively on Amazon e.g. Used clothes
2. Visually appealing collectibles benefit from more photos and more detailed descriptions
3. When you think that an eBay auction setting may yield many bids and possibly a higher price than a set price Amazon listing
4. When Amazon's shipping allowance does not cover actual shipping costs – set your own shipping fees on your eBay auction.
5. When you want money fast. eBay auctions end in 1,3,5, or 7 days (10 days at a higher list price).

Amazon Fba: An Introduction To Fulfillment By Amazon

All experienced internet sellers today are talking about Amazon FBA and for good reason. FBA allows business owners to scale up their business and sell large volumes of goods quickly. It also eliminates some of the overhead issues associated with selling on Amazon with a Merchant Fulfilled (MF) account, like item storage and packing and shipping individual items.

FBA sellers also have definite advantages over MF sellers. The biggest advantage is that all FBA items on Amazon are available for purchase by Amazon Prime members, with free two-day shipping. There are getting to be more and more Prime members. People don't want to wait for their orders anymore and Prime gets them their orders FAST and they also get Amazon's customer care, which is another advantage. Many Prime members ONLY buy items that are available with Prime shipping, which means FBA sellers get a ton of orders from Prime members.

I sell a large percentage of my items through FBA now and probably 75% of my orders are from Prime members. You can tell which orders are Amazon Prime orders because Prime orders display in your Amazon Seller account as having 'Second Day' shipping.

FBA sellers get another huge advantage because FBA listings are much more likely to win the Buy Box and show up first on each Amazon sales page, because of their affiliation with Amazon Prime shipping. Even if your item is priced well above the lowest MF price, Amazon will display items that are available through Prime (FBA) in the Buy Box. That's awesome for FBA sellers – items displayed in the Buy Box sell considerably faster and you can get higher sales prices, as well.

To make a long story short, items listed through FBA sell considerably faster and at higher listing prices than MF items. That's why many veteran Amazon sellers end up graduating to FBA after selling with a MF account for a while.

Still, FBA is not for everybody. You can't just say, "FBA looks cool. I'm going to start selling on FBA tomorrow!"

No, no, no. It's not that simple, my friend.

Selling on FBA is much more technical than selling with a MF account and you also have considerable start-up costs to get going. Thank goodness for that! Otherwise, everybody would be selling on FBA and the competition would be terrible.

First, there is a learning curve to selling on FBA. When I started, I read all of the FBA help pages and ordered several books on selling on FBA on Kindle. I also watched a number of FBA-related YouTube videos. That really helped prepare me for selling on FBA. Still, the first couple of shipments to FBA were a bit stressful.

Amazon has a strict set of rules that FBA sellers must follow when they prepare to ship items to Amazon to make them available through FBA. The manner in which each type of item must be packaged is outlined in the FBA help pages. If boxes or items are received that don't meet Amazon specifications, they are not processed. So, they are either discarded at the warehouse and you lose everything that you messed up on, or you have to pay to have everything shipped back to you. You can see where it is vital to prepare shipments correctly the first time.

Here is the link to the [Amazon FBA Help Pages](#).

As I mentioned before, in order to compete consistently with other FBA sellers, you are going to have to shell out some cash and buy some equipment and supplies in order to prepare shipments for the Amazon warehouses. Some of this equipment you may already have from shipping MF orders, but most of it will have to be bought before you start selling on FBA.

Minimum starting equipment that you will need:

Shrink Wrap (Buy in Bulk)

Thick packing tape and strapping tape (Buy in Bulk)

Large Boxes (You can re-use old boxes to ship to FBA, but if you use the same sized boxes all the time, you can streamline the shipping process greatly)

Clear Shipping Cling Wrap (This comes in large rolls and is used for wrapping large items like toys that are required to be sealed before shipment)

Fragile and Child Danger stickers (These are required for some items)

An Electronic Postal Scale that will weigh boxes up to 70 LBs

A Laser Printer that prints high quality labels – FBA requires you to label many items and these labels MUST be of a certain quality, or the items will not be accepted.

30-Up Labels (Buy in Bulk)

Impulse Sealer and Heat Gun (Highly Recommended)

You can see that there are investments in both research time and buying equipment to start selling on FBA. But, sellers can definitely upgrade their businesses by utilizing FBA.

After I got approved for my FBA account, I started by shipping in a lot of my smaller media items that I had listed for sale in my MF account. This process is very easy. All you have to do is go into your inventory and click on 'Edit' next to the item that you want to ship to FBA and then click on 'Shipped by Amazon'.

I shipped several boxes of CDs, DVDs and Cassettes into FBA and I was very surprised when I was able to list the items sometimes $10 higher and they still sold when the items were made available through FBA. In addition, the items sold a lot faster. I sold several media items that had been available for over three years in my MF inventory in only several months on FBA.

I have steadily moved more and more items to FBA, including larger items like toys, video game systems and housewares.

You do have to be careful not to get carried away with FBA. It is tempting to send EVERYTHING in and let Amazon handle all of the packing and shipping. But, there are some items that are easier and more cost-effective to handle with your MF account.

For instance, large and/or heavy items are usually better off being sold MF. FBA charges significant storage and fulfillment fees for items that are deemed to be 'Oversized'. Some of these items are not really very large, so you have to be careful to check and see that items are not considered oversized before you ship them in to FBA.

There are also some types of items are also not allowed to be sold through FBA. I have tried to list a number of items like DVDs and CDs that FBA would not take, because of their strange warning system, which somehow makes random items look like Hazardous items. I eventually either listed them MF, or built a new Amazon page for the items using a new UPC number purchased through eBay.

Many sellers also prefer to not ship fragile items like glass housewares and vinyl records in to FBA. These items are difficult to prepare for shipment to Amazon and you also have to rely on FBA warehouse workers to pack and ship these items correctly (they sometimes use poor packing materials and containers). I have quite a few of these types of items that I have kept in my MF inventory and have not sent them in to FBA. I want to package these items myself. I don't want to risk the cost of shipping the items to Amazon and have the items not make it there, or even worse, have an item get purchased and then get refunded because of breakage.

There are many other tasks that you will have to accomplish when you start selling on FBA and you will learn as you go. Each shipment that you send to FBA gets easier and faster and before you know it, you are a pro.

TREND NOTE: Amazon just announced that new FBA sellers will not be able to send in shipments to Amazon fulfillment center until January 2017. That's bad news for new sellers hoping to jump in to Q4 2016 sales hikes, but good news for existing FBA sellers. For the new folks, the extra couple of months gives you time to get your business plan developed, source inventory and get your FBA labeling and packaging techniques mastered.

We will go much more in-depth on the step-by-step process of listing, packing and shipping items to FBA in an upcoming book dedicated to that subject.

Retail Arbitrage [Ra]

WARNING: There are a number of blogs talking about the "end of RA/OA in 2017". They are saying that Amazon is planning on restricting the use of retail store receipts as proof that inventory is legitimate, instead requiring invoices directly from manufacturers to be able to sell products on FBA. This would make the RA system much more labor-intensive.

These blogs are also warning sellers that Amazon may forbid sellers from selling products bought from retail stores as New. Instead, they would have to sell those items intended to be sold under the RA system as 'Used – Like New'. If true, this would basically blow up the whole RA system on Amazon and would require sales on other sites like eBay. Do your research, folks.

Retail arbitrage is defined as the practice of buying goods at a physical retail store like Costco and then flipping the same items for profit by offering them for sale online on websites like Amazon.

The main difference between thrift store arbitrage and retail arbitrage is that the cost of the goods that you buy is considerably higher when bought at a retail store. Therefore, you have to be a lot more careful about what you buy at retail stores. You will generally also have a lower profit margin for each item sold, so you have to pay more attention to overhead costs to ensure that you actually earn at least a minimum amount of profit for each item. You don't want to put in hours sourcing inventory and listing and shipping it to Amazon to actually deposit only 89 cents per item into your bank account.

Don't laugh. It's happened to everybody that sells with the retail arbitrage system. Here's how it happens... You see a great close-out bargain on Halloween light systems on November 1 at Wal-Mart. You price check the item and even if you price match the item at the lowest FBA offering, you will still earn over $16 per item. Score!

So, you buy all 15 of the lighting systems. You list them two days later and the lowest FBA price has dropped $3 because they are available throughout the whole Wal-Mart chain in the US at the same price. Crap.

You list the systems and send them in to FBA at $13 profit/item. By the time the systems get to the fulfillment center and are made available for sale, the price has come down another $1. You adjust your Amazon price accordingly. The lowest FBA price continues to drop as the item is offered by dozens of FBA sellers.

You hold steady with your price, thinking that some of the other FBA sellers will run out of product and you will be able to sell yours at the higher price soon. Meanwhile, the product gets two bad reviews on Amazon because the product is Wal-Mart junk and sales rank goes into the tank, which means it does not show up as often in search results.

You finally end up lowering your price almost to the break-even point the next July and finally sell your products, after eating a long-term storage fee and other fees for months. You consider yourself lucky not to lose money on the purchase.

This type of scenario occurs regularly with retail arbitrage. It's the dark side of the business that the "I made $14 million on Amazon FBA" books and videos intentionally avoid.

The point is, with retail arbitrage, there is an inherent risk associated with the system. With thrift arbitrage, you often have a very low purchase price per item and you only have one or two of each inventory item. If the item does not sell for a while, it's no big deal.

With retail arbitrage, you have to understand the FBA business to be successful. I equate retail arbitrage to the stock market. Yes, you can make a crap-load of money in the stock market… IF you know what the hell you are doing. If you DON'T understand the stock market, you can lose your shirt quickly. The same is true of retail arbitrage.

It's easy to find deals that look great and SHOULD earn you a great paycheck. Yet, if you don't know what it actually costs to get the items shipped to FBA and what FBA is going to charge in storage fees if your items don't sell immediately, you will earn at best, a minimal monthly salary.

That's why a lot of retail arbitrage sellers do not work full-time selling on Amazon. There are definitely some RA sellers that earn hundreds of thousands of dollars a year in profit. But those people are the ones that work the hardest, do the most research and experiment with business systems to find out what works in their area. Most people don't have the work ethic or the free time to commit to go full time. If you are one of the few people who are willing to work hard and smart, you can make a lot of money in the RA system.

So, how do I get into the RA game, you ask?

First, you need to get a modern smart phone, if you don't have one. Any one will do, although I am partial to Android phones over iCrap phones. Download a suitable Amazon price scanner app. There are quite a few different options, including some decent free apps.

You will definitely want to download the free Amazon Seller App. It allows you to scan items to price check them, manage your inventory, check your seller messages and see your orders. You will use this app often.

Another good free app is the standard Amazon app, which allows you to quickly scan or check the price and reviews of an item. I actually use this often for doing a quick price scan, if I don't need in-depth sales price history. It's very user friendly.

Amazon FBA calculator is a free webpage that allows you to check the FBA fees, so you can figure out your ROI (Return on Investment) for a potential inventory item. You can bookmark this page, so that you can access it quickly.

Camelcamelcamel.com is one website that provides current and historical Amazon prices. They also have the Camelizer Chrome extension, which allows you to check prices directly from any major retailer website for free. I use the extension quite a bit to check history before major purchases.

[Price Bandit](#) is another RA seller favorite. It's another price scan / price history app available on Android and IOS. This app has changed several times lately. It used to have a free trial period, but I believe that now you have to pay a modest fee (about $15) to use it. Many RA veterans swear by this app.

Inventory Lab and Scoutify is another very popular app. Inventory Lab ($49/mo.) allows you to manage your inventory and re-price items as other sellers try to undercut you. Scoutify is the price scanner app that is provided for free for IL customers. Many RA sellers LOVE Scoutify and use it as their primary go-to sourcing app.

Many other sellers use apps like the Groupon app and Retail Me Not to find items to sell and get discount coupon codes to reduce costs and increase ROI.

Many RA sellers use a dedicated mobile scanner like the ScanFob, which allows you to scan faster, more accurately and also scan hard-to-read bar codes. It is also very helpful to have a USB bar code scanner, which allows you to scan bar codes from your laptop or desktop computer when you are at home listing items. These USB scanners can be found for $20-30 on eBay and Amazon and will save you a ton of time over the life of your business.

How To Succeed In Ra

Tips for RA sellers could easily fill an entire book, but here are some of the most important tips:

1. Customer feedback is extremely important, especially for beginning sellers. Do everything in your power to get positive feedbacks and avoid negatives. Amazon is much more restrictive than eBay or other similar sites. Negative feedback can quickly lead to your selling account being suspended. Feedback approval under 95% will also prevent you from being approved to sell toys during the holiday season (for non-FBA sellers) and also getting approval to sell in gated categories. Consider using a feedback management app like Feedback Genius to keep your feedback percentages high. When you receive negative or neutral feedback, always attempt to rectify the situation with the customer – whatever it takes!
2. Understand Amazon FBA fees and how they affect your ROI. There are fairly substantial long term storage fees charged for items that do not sell quickly and the fess are higher for larger items because it costs more for Amazon warehouses to store the items. You can offset these fees by buying items that have high sales rank and will move quickly. You will also pay considerably less storage fees for small, light items. Small, light items are

also much cheaper to ship in to Amazon and they cost less to package them, as well.

3. Use the tools available to you. Amazon sales rank by itself often does not tell you what you need to know when you are considering buying a larger quantity of items. Use apps like camelcamelcamel to get the whole sales picture and make important decisions.

4. Get Amazon-approval for gated categories as soon as possible. There are thousands of products that you can sell without applying for approval, but some of the most profitable categories are gated to prevent rookie sellers from accidentally selling counterfeit products and/or reducing the quality of offerings on Amazon. Categories like groceries, collectible books, beauty and cosmetics, clothes, watches and major appliances are examples of gated categories. You can see a full list here. There is a good walk-through on how to get approved for certain categories here. They all require that you are a Pro Merchant Amazon seller.

5. Be flexible. Be able to source in several different categories and get familiar with many different stores. Be wary of sourcing from the most popular retail stores like Wal Mart and Meijer. You can find good items to source at those stores, but often, sales are running concurrently nationwide. So, items that look great end up having a ton of competition within a week, driving prices down quickly. Look for out-of-the way stores to source from. Some favorite chain stores are Costco, Big Lots and IKEA.

Also, look for foreign stores, specialty shops, thrift stores than sell new items and "Mom and Pop" non-chain stores.
6. Treat your RA business as a business! Keep your overhead as low as possible. Consider hiring an accountant and tax professional, as soon as you can. Keep track of receipts and plan for income tax season. Use a business checking account to keep your affairs in order.
7. Identify businesses that offer "percent back" or rebate cards. Use business credit cards to rack up frequent flyer miles, but ALWAYS pay off your cards each month to avoid paying interest fees. Know when stores run their specials and plan accordingly.
8. Just start doing it! Don't be intimidated by the process. If others can do it, so can you. Start raking cash, ASAP!

Introduction To Wholesaling And Private Label Products [Plp]

Wholesaling and private label products are two different forms of arbitrage that involve finding products that are already being sold or manufactured and offering them for a higher price on Amazon to earn profit.

Wholesaling is finding items that are being produced in scale elsewhere, buying a defined number of units (usually at least 100 item shipments) and then making an item page on Amazon, so that you can make profit on each sale.

Private label products are like a specialized version of wholesale items. With private label products, you find a source of low-cost goods, add specialized branding and/or packaging and then make a new listing on Amazon, so that you can raise the selling price enough to make a good ROI on the purchase. Often, with PLP, you work with the manufacturer to have your logo, brand and possibly packaging applied to their generic product.

Both of these methods are extremely hot right now with Amazon sellers, because if you find the right products - or even better, line of products, you can make a lot of money quickly.

The **advantages** of PLP and wholesaling:

1. Scale – you can add a lot of inventory items very quickly
2. Easy to list, package and ship to FBA. This is a big one. Once you find a good product, all you have to do is replenish your inventory and then you package and ship exactly the same way every time, using the same labels and boxes. This reduces your time spent per item, as well as overhead cost, because you can buy supplies in bulk. You can even arrange to have your item shipped directly from your manufacturer to FBA, if you are good!
3. If you hit the sweet spot, you can make a lot of money very quickly. If you find an item that has no competition and existing demand on Amazon, you can sell out your inventory in no time. Of course, finding those products takes both a lot of work and some luck.
4. Utilizes Amazon's brand to bring internet traffic and increase orders. If you tried to only sell these types of items on your own website, you may have a hard time getting enough internet traffic to consistently sell products. But, listing the same product on Amazon exposes your product to the #1 internet marketplace in the world. Plus, Amazon has an excellent reputation for offering quality products and a very good customer service department. Most people are comfortable ordering goods from Amazon. And, because you are an FBA seller, you also have the advantage of your item

being available via Amazon Prime. This allows you to sell your item at higher prices and faster sales rates.

The **challenges** of selling wholesale items and PLP:

1. Competition. Like we previously discussed, everybody and their brother (and sister) is looking for good wholesale items to sell on Amazon right now. Therefore, it is hard to find new innovative products and the profit margins are smaller for items that have other existing Amazon listings.
2. There is a lot of leg work involved in the process of finding products and making them available on for sale on Amazon. It's not easy to find products that will consistently retain a high enough price to earn a good profit. You have to have good business sense. You must be able to estimate the potential for increased competition and decide if products will be profitable, if you have to lower sales price due to competition. You will have to use profit estimating apps and/or web pages to determine ROI. This is much more important with these systems than with thrift arbitrage, or even retail arbitrage. You also have to communicate with manufacturers to line up products, determine amounts and apply private label branding. And then, there is time and effort to make a great Amazon listing and ensure that you get some good customer reviews for your item(s).

3. There is more risk. There is no way around this one. With these systems, there is more inherent risk with trying to sell new private products. Until you have made a fair amount of sales on Amazon, you don't know for sure if your item will sell consistently at your asking price. You also don't know how customer will like the products. If new products get more than one or two poor reviews, they are almost impossible to sell after that, unless sales rank is already high. Although most companies will allow you order a "trial shipment" of 50 or 100 items, you still run the risk of losing much of your investment, if the items do not sell as you anticipated. You also have to consider the strong possibility that you will accrue FBA long term storage (LTS) fees, if competition increases or you get a negative feedback or two. LTS fees can really cut into your projected profit estimates.
4. You have to be able to make professional looking Amazon sales pages to be successful with these systems. This is difficult for many beginning Amazon sellers and honestly, you should also invest in some equipment to do the job right. You can't just create an Amazon sales page in five minutes and expect it to perform well over time. We will talk more about this task shortly.

How To Succeed In Wholesale And Plp Systems

It would be easy to discuss methods for increasing profit in these systems for over 100 pages, but that is beyond the scope of this book.

But, there some general ideas that all wholesale and PLP sellers use that you should be familiar with, in order to sell these goods consistently and earn your minimum allowable ROI.

The first and most important rule is that you must have a business model that guides your buying and selling practices. You have to determine for yourself what you minimum allowable ROI is going to be for each product. Most sellers are looking for items that have an ROI of around 100%. This is also called the "3X rule", because you are looking to buy sales inventory at $5 per item and then flip it on Amazon, at a price of $15. This allows you to earn a minimum profit, after budgeting for the cost of getting the item to FBA, along with the associated selling and storage fees.

Of course, a 100% ROI is not easy to find, especially for beginning sellers, so YOU need to determine what your acceptable ROI and risk factors (sales rank, etc.) are going to be. Once you establish your business model, be strict in your adherence to your numbers. Don't increase risk by "taking a flyer" on a product that does not meet your specs.

For wholesale and PLP systems, it is vital to get the generic products at a very low cost. Often, sellers are sourcing wholesale products from overseas, or buying them through wholesale aggregator websites like Alibaba.

One of the best ways to reduce overhead costs is to avoid the middle man and go straight to the source and deal with the manufacturer via their company website. This allows you get lower prices per item, arrange private label branding, reduce minimum 'item per shipment' requirements and get more information on their products. Sometimes, you can even special order a particular color or minor design changes to suit your needs.

By far the most important aspect of selling wholesale and PLPs is making an effective Amazon sales page and getting traffic to the page via Amazon SEO. The single most important part of the sales page is the main photograph of the product. Yet, many private label products have terrible, blurry photos that scream "inferior product".

It is vital that your photograph looks as good as every other product that you are competing against. Often, that means making a small investment to make that happen. You can either pay a professional photographer to take a series of photos of your product, or if you have some skill, you can take a quality photo yourself with a good camera and light box.

It is definitely worth studying up on how to take great photographs for sales. And, every penny that you spend will be returned to you many times over in sales over the life of your product.

Keywords and Search Engine Optimization (SEO) are also important aspects of the sales page. There are many ways to research keywords and determine traffic generation of phrases related to your product. You can check keywords for free with the Google Adwords tool, as long as you set up a free account with Google Ads.

Once you determine which keywords are most relevant to your product, you should insert the keyword phrases into your title and item description, as Amazon uses both of these locations to decide which products are displayed to customers after search queries.

Your item description should also be well written, concise and, for God's sake, spell check and grammar check your text. Sheesh! I've looked at hundreds of these products and it is amazing how many of them you can look at and immediately tell that the sales page was made by an individual and not a manufacturer.

Spend the time and money necessary to put your product on par with every other major product listed on Amazon.

Introduction To Drop Shipping

Drop shipping is, in essence, an extension of wholesaling. It is also a viable alternative to Amazon FBA for many internet sellers, who already have an internet presence and can utilize a website, blog, large social media following, or a sizeable email list to generate traffic. With drop shipping, you arrange to have a third party company fulfill orders for you and ship sold items from their holding facilities directly to customers.

Here is the run-down on how drop shipping works. Step 1, you find a wholesale seller and make arrangements to sell a line of products (or a single product). Step 2, you make sales pages to sell the product on various sites, including making an item listing on Amazon (remember, you must have a Professional Seller account to make a listing on Amazon). You can also make a fixed price listing on eBay for the same products. Most drop shippers also drive traffic to their sales pages from outside websites, blogs, social media ads and email lists.

When customers place an order from Amazon, you collect the Amazon sales price, plus the Amazon shipping credit. You pay the drop shipping company their lower whole sale price and their shipping fee per item. You earn profit with each sale with internet arbitrage – finding low cost items and selling at higher prices via Amazon or eBay.

Advantages of drop shipping:

1. Amazon and eBay are free sources of internet traffic. They are the largest internet retailers in the world and will generate sales by themselves, which reduces the amount of paid advertising you have to use.
2. Semi-passive income – once you have the arrangements made, shipping is taken care of and you don't do much besides monitor the effectiveness of listings and keywords and perhaps do some outside advertisements and blog posting.
3. You don't pay for products until they sell, which reduces risk. You do not have to buy large amounts of wholesale products and ship them to Amazon FBA warehouses.
4. You can easily diversify your product line and establish a niche, by offering groups of similar products to a defined market. This makes it easier to bring traffic to your products by building a website or blog that caters to your market.

Disadvantages of drop shipping:

1. You don't control the shipping practices of the drop shipping company. This can lead to breakage loss, negative feedbacks and you cannot add your own branding to the packages. There have been numerous problems reported by internet sellers regarding shoddy packaging by drop shipping companies. As you might guess, these companies try to save money by using cheap packaging

materials. You will not see top quality boxes or cushioning products used by these drop shippers.
2. There are many scams out there. You have to be very careful to ensure that the drop shipping company is legitimate. Don't even think about using drop shippers that offer free sign-ups. There is going to be a cost for using their service. Only use high profile companies and verify performance by going on social media (like Facebook internet sellers groups) and talking to sellers that use the services.
3. You have to really watch your inventory levels. Drop shippers are order fulfillers. They do not manage your Amazon account, so they don't know when your inventory runs out. This is really a problem when you have listings on multiple sites. You have to monitor your inventory and make sure that you don't have orders placed that you cannot fulfill, or you risk negative feedbacks and possible suspension.
4. As with wholesaling, finding products that make acceptable profit margins through drop shipping companies can be time consuming and tedious. You also have to work with the companies to ensure quality products are delivered to your customers and quickly cut ties with underperforming suppliers.

There are really two main types of websites that offer drop shipping services. The easiest way to get started is to find an aggregator that offers large selections of products.

These types of websites generally are easy to find and set up arrangements, but offer significantly lower profit margins, as they are essentially middle-men.

The second way to use this system is to arrange drop shipping directly from the manufacturer and cut out the middle man. This system increases profits, but there can be more legwork required to find these companies.

I cannot make personal recommendations for which drop shippers are best, as I do not utilize this system, but there is a ton of information online (like my kids say… Google it) and you can get a lot of good information from experienced sellers the drop ship on Facebook groups.

Preparing To Succeed On Amazon In The Future: Amazon Selling Trends And What They Mean For You

One thing is for certain, Amazon is the leading online retail website for a reason. They stay current with internet shopping behavior by offering cutting edge sales page features on its site in order to entice buyers to order from Amazon.

Therefore, Amazon is constantly rolling out new display features and catering to customers' appetites. Amazon sellers must routinely research Amazon News and seller forums to stay ahead of a competitive field.

TREND 1: Going Global. Amazon has recently launched Unified Global accounts for North America and Europe. North American Global accounts allow Amazon sellers to concurrently list products on Amazon US, Canada and Mexico for Merchant Fulfilled listings. It is important to note that FBA listings can NOT share inventory across all three Amazon sites. Instead, FBA listings can only be fulfilled in the FBA center it is sent to. In other words, Canadian FBA items would only be available via Amazon.ca, not Amazon.com. There is also a Unified account for European sellers (all 5 major Amazon sites in Europe are included)

So, this is great news for MF sellers. All you have to do is request approval for each additional site and within several days, you can your MF inventory available in all three North American Amazon sites. The unified accounts each keep their metrics separate, so a negative feedback from a Canadian buyer through Amazon.ca would not affect your .com or .mx accounts.

For FBA sellers, the NA Unified account does allow you to diversify your products, but you are required to send in separate shipments to each marketplace's fulfillment center. When you sign up, you can also vary the Canada or Mexico price from your US listing price by a set amount or a set percentage, which can help to offset international shipping costs (Amazon shipping allowances do not always cover actual shipping costs for products shipped outside the US).

You can either click on the link to apply for approval for a NA Unified account, or most sellers can click on a link titled 'Expanding Internationally on Amazon' from their Seller Central page.

TREND 2: Amazon is really cracking down on reviews that are perceived as potentially being arranged or paid for by third party sellers. The days of gaming the system and paying for product reviews or having people you know jack up your positive reviews are numbered.

Rumors are flying amongst elite third party PLP Amazon sellers that the company will shortly make Amazon Vine reviews available to third party private label products, where it used to only be available to Amazon Vendor Central manufacturers (first party sellers that sell directly to Amazon).

You can bet that Amazon will offer Vine review approval to the sellers with the best seller metrics, so strive for exceptional customer approval numbers. By all means, if you get invited to participate in Vine, take advantage of it.

Vine reviews are high profile reviews that are accepted unconditionally as authentic by most customers.

TREND 3: Competition will make Amazon Sponsored Ads necessary to keep pace with other sellers that are paying to create new customers and elevate the amount of traffic to their products on Amazon. You may as well start researching the best way to utilize Sponsored Ads now.

Sponsored Ads in Amazon's "Pay to Play" system, where sellers pay for traffic by setting an amount that they will pay for each click directed to their particular Amazon item listing.

Amazon does currently have a $50 credit for new Sponsored Ads sellers, as long as that $50 is used by January 1, 2017.

TREND 4: Seller Fulfilled Prime. This is an enticing new offering from Amazon that allows select sellers to enroll in a program that makes their products available to Prime customers (and thereby often get the Buy Box), WITHOUT selling on Amazon FBA.

As you might guess, Amazon is very selective about which sellers are allowed to participate in this program. This is only for medium to high volume sellers, not beginners – there is a trial period of up to 90 days. During the trial period, the seller must maintain a 99% On Time

Delivery percentage and a Defect rate of <1% across a minimum of 200 Prime orders.

This program necessitates the use of an arranged shipping service, as all Prime orders must be received within 2 days of customer order. Standard USPS or UPS shipping will not be adequate for most sellers, especially those sellers that utilize USPS Media mail for books, music, movies, etc.

TREND 5: VIDEO. Amazon is considering using short video content for 3rd party sellers in secondary photos, according to some sources. If this comes to fruition, those sellers that have video uploaded to their product pages will have a considerable advantage, so keep your eye out for this update.

Which System Should I Use?

There are many factors that will ultimately determine which system will be most satisfying and profitable for your own internet selling situation:

1. The time and money that you have available to devote to your Amazon business
2. Experience levels and internet sales skill
3. Availability of sourcing locations in your area
4. Local competition
5. Skill in running an internet business
6. Willingness to spend hours of time on tedious tasks like looking at hundreds of potentially profitable wholesale products and making inventory and shipping arrangements with these wholesale companies.
7. Personal preferences regarding what you enjoy selling most – many Amazon sellers just enjoy the search for second-hand treasure and the challenge of finding individual items that sell for huge profit margins. Others are only trying to maximize monthly income through volume of sales.

One thing is for sure. As with any other venture, if you have limited experience selling goods online, you should get familiar with the processes before you dive in headfirst. For most internet sellers, this means starting out by "testing the waters" with relatively low risk systems like thrift arbitrage (TA) and retail arbitrage (RA). These systems allow you to secure inventory that consistently sells for good profit levels, without having to make large investments that could fail.

TA and RA systems also give you a chance to be more involved in the listing and fulfillment processes, so that you see for yourself how Amazon fees and packaging and shipping costs affect your bottom line profits over time.

Many beginning internet sellers take the same path toward building a large successful Amazon business that I took a long time ago:

1. Do a lot of research about how to sell effectively on Amazon. Look at what types of items and source inventory sell well and that you are interested in selling.
2. Begin by selling items with Merchant Fulfilled (MF) Amazon account. First sell free items that are already at your home or family's homes (unwanted items, like books that you have already read, CDs you don't want anymore, or outgrown toys, etc.). Then, start buying local products to sell at second-hand and retail locations that you can sell on Amazon. You can also easily add internet arbitrage inventory, like large wholesale eBay auctions for media items.
3. After you have built a sustainable Amazon inventory and are selling more than 40 items a month, upgrade to an Amazon Professional Seller account. This allows you to create sales pages on Amazon and explore other selling systems, like FBA.

4. Start exploring ways to increase the scale of your business. This can involve buying larger lots of items at retail stores or adding wholesale products. You would also be looking to expand your presence by building an outside website, getting social media traffic and building an email list to drive traffic to your Amazon store inventory.
5. Determine how you want to run your business long-term. Do you want to big-time and sell on Amazon full-time? Do you prefer to keep your business fun and want to keep your traditional job and supplement that income by selling used items part-time? Are you ready to really go for it and make an investment in time and money to build a full-scale internet business that includes Amazon via drop shipping or private label products?

I will conclude this book the same way that I do with most of my other books, with this advice. YOU HAVE TO START RIGHT NOW.

Don't just "think about it". Don't say "I'll start next week, or next month". You will never start doing it and you will miss out on a huge opportunity!

Start selling items right now! Don't be one of those people that are afraid to try something new. Yes, I'm talking to you. Register for your Amazon seller account now. Look around your house for something to sell. Find a book or CD that has a bar code. List it on Amazon. Congratulations! It's as easy as that. Rinse and repeat. Keep listing items.

You are up and running. Woo hoo! Now, you just have to wait a short time for the money to start rolling in, while you relax and do whatever it is that you like to do.

Additional Links For Further Research

Eric Michael Author Central Page

'Almost Free Money' books for Internet Resellers:

1) Almost Free Money, Volume 1 FREE! (#1 Kindle bestseller, Top 10 for 3 years running). Learn how to find over 500 different types of items for free where you live and sell for profit online and at scrap metal locations for big bucks.

2) Thrift Wars (#1 Kindle Bestseller): Learn how professional sellers locate the best items to resell from thrift stores for very high profit margins. Learn how to sell on Amazon, Etsy and eBay for maximum profit margins.

3) Etsy Empire (#1 Kindle and Softcover bestseller, top 10 for 8 months straight): How to build a powerful Etsy shop and sell handmade and collectible items on Etsy.com. Master Etsy SEO, social media for Etsy and Etsy marketing with a proven step-by-step formula.

4) Etsy Empire Strikes Back (#1 Kindle Bestseller): Advanced techniques for marketing with social media, like Facebook, Instagram and Pinterest, plus the latest Etsy shop rules and updates

5) Almost Free Gold: (#1 Kindle bestseller, top 10 for 12 months straight): Learn how to find valuable gold and silver jewelry for cheap at garage sales and thrift stores. You can also learn how to harvest free gold and silver from junk sources in this fun and unique approach to earning income!

6) The Almost Free Money Triple Play Value Pack: Contains the three bestselling AFM books: Almost Free Money, Passive Income for Life and Garage Sale Superstar. A great bargain!

7) Fast Cash: Selling Used Items for Profit: (#1 Kindle and Softcover bestseller) Learn how to find the best items at second-hand locations and build your own business on Amazon, eBay and Etsy.

8) Garage Sale Superstar: (#1 Kindle bestseller and Top 10 for 12 months): Learn how to make the most profit possible at your next garage sale. Tips on organizing, advertising and pricing at garage sales, yard sales and estate sales.

Thank You, Readers!

Thank you for taking the time to read this book. I hope that you enjoyed it as much as I enjoyed writing it.

Please put your mind to immediately applying what you learned in this book. Don't wait until next week to start! You can find items to sell in any location, and at any time of the year.

YOU have to make up your mind to start selling used items on Amazon, and it will be all increasing profits from there. I wish you success in building your passive income through Amazon.

Click on the link below to join the Almost Free Money Nation. This free newsletter provides exclusive free white papers and advance reading chapters from unreleased AFM books, free tips and tricks to help you find great items at second-locations and learn how to sell them, and links to new Garage Sale Academy webpages.

http://forms.aweber.com/form/75/228725575.htm

If you have any questions, please contact me at the Almost Free Money Facebook page, on Twitter, or email me at almostfreemoney@yahoo.com. I would enjoy hearing from you!

If you feel that this book has helped you to find new and enjoyable ways to make a new passive income for you and your family, I humbly ask you for only two things. #1, tell your family and friends about this book, and #2, please take several seconds to leave positive feedback for this book on its Amazon Detail Page. After all, you should be able to easily make 1000 times the $3 that you spent on this book in your first year of selling.

Positive feedback directly affects other readers' reviews and leads to additional orders, and the proceeds from this book will go directly into my sons' college funds. Thanks again, and happy hunting!

Thrift Wars: A Battle-Tested Internet Business Plan: Find Hidden Thrift Stores Treasure and Sell on Amazon, eBay and Etsy for Huge Profits with Online Arbitrage is now updated on Amazon Kindle.

Thrift Wars is the first true Thrift Store flipping manual and includes hands-on experience finding a huge variety of thrift store items and selling them for maximum profit on eBay, Amazon, Amazon FBA, Etsy and Classified sites.

Topics: The best thrifts to shop, how to buy low and sell high, maximizing per-item profit, improving online listings and photos on eBay and Amazon, diversification across multiple internet sales venues, identification of high-end collectibles and sales items, locating gold and silver at thrift shops and much more. The book is illustrated with rescued thrift store treasures and their online sales prices.

Readers' Praise for Almost Free Money

5.0 out of 5 stars

The author is a money-making machine

By **Bill Nelson**

This review is from: **Almost Free Money: How to Make Extra Money on Free Items That You Can Find Anywhere, Including Garage Sales, Thrift Shops, Scrap Metal and Finding Gold (Kindle Edition)**

"This guy is like a money-making machine. Almost Free Money: How to Make Significant Money on Free Items That You Can Find Anywhere, Including Garage Sales, Scrap Metal, and Discarded Items by Eric Michael is yet another goldmine of information on how to make money!

Seriously, whether you want to earn some extra cash in your spare time or want to make a career out of buying and selling, this book (and several others by the same author) will get you going, and keep you there. The appendix is worth the price of the book but every page contains valuable tips and pointers. Highly recommended 5-stars."

5.0 out of 5 stars

This is a great book! It contains lots of ideas on how to make money from surprising places

By **Steven Johnson "Publisher of debt and credit"**

Amazon Seller Academy

This review is from: Almost Free Money: How to Make Extra Money on Free Items That You Can Find Anywhere, Including Garage Sales, Thrift Shops, Scrap Metal and Finding Gold (Kindle Edition)

"This is a great book! It contains lots of ideas on how to make money from surprising places, and the resource directory at the back of the book is worth 10x the price of this book all by itself. Highly recommended. I like the way the author told how he got started in this type of business, and his advice on what to sell as scrap, what to sell as collectible, and what to sell as utilitarian, everyday use, was very interesting. I'm sure that as I visit thrift shops and garage sales in the future, this book will help me identify many new items that will make me money!"

Readers' Praise for Almost Free Gold!

5.0 out of 5 stars **Informative and very helpful!**

Sammy K. (Galveston, TX)

This review is from: Almost Free Gold!: How to Earn a Quick $1000 Finding Gold, Silver and Platinum Where You Live (Almost Free Money) (Kindle Edition)

"I have been picking at yard sales and thrift stores for years and have used several of the other books in this series with success, including Almost Free

Money. I learned a lot that I didn't know from Almost Free Gold. For me, the most valuable portions of the book were the methods for finding hidden gold and sterling at yard sales. I've got lots of new places to look and now I know how to find the stuff that other pickers have missed! I am also planning on taking the author's advice and contacting some of the businesses mentioned for setting up consistent sources of precious metals. Plus, you have to check out the chapter on the metal that is more valuable than gold! Fascinating stuff and the basis for a new hobby / business / addiction combination!"

www.ingramcontent.com/pod-product-compliance
Lightning Source LLC
Chambersburg PA
CBHW061146180526
45170CB00002B/644